If you're looking for honesty and vulnerability, this collection will give you both. A beautiful book of growth and self-love.

- Alexandra Elle, Author of *After the Rain*

As you work through cultivating a more powerful and meaningful relationship with yourself, Things You Need To Hear Most is a perfect companion. Samukele speaks directly to the soul and spirit as she describes and shares the process of coming home to ourselves and as we learn to trust ourselves to be so much more than we ever could have imagined. These poems are necessary reading for anyone looking to deepen their relationship to self, and to their own truth.

- Komal Minhas, Interviewer + Educator

Things You Need to Hear Most

Things You Need to Hear Most

A collection
of poetry and notes,
rooted in self-love

by Samukele Ncube

Things You Need to Hear Most
Copyright © 2021 by Samukele Ncube.

All rights reserved. No part of this book may be reproduced or used in any manner without written permission of the copyright owner except for the use of quotations in a book review.
For more information, email: sam@samukelencube.com

Book Cover Design by Samukele Ncube
Book Design by Jessica Slater
Interior Illustrations by Anastasiya Dzi
First Edition

ISBN: 978-1-7774452-0-1

www.samukelencube.com

*For the past versions of me who
needed to hear this.*

Acknowledgments

For a long time, I felt community meant a sea of people together. Now, I am coming to realize that community can be found in a few people or even one person.

It is a shared intimacy with someone that allows you to be seen, heard, and accepted. It is the people who make you feel at home, and free to be yourself, wholly.

Where you are not playing a role to suit who others need you to be, but where your true self is celebrated - flaws and all - with no judgement.

Where you can laugh and cry in the same breath; where you can share the parts of yourself that you have cast to the shadows and find unconditional love; where hours pass and it feels like you have just gotten started.

There aren't enough words to describe this feeling; it is home.

My community is the reason this book exists today, and it is because of these special humans that I had the strength and courage to keep going, thank you for being my home.

To my mom, thank you for teaching me resilience, and dad, thank you for encouraging me along my journey of self-exploration. To my sister Tanya, thank you for always reminding me to be the light I want to see in the world; to my friends, Christie and Rita, thank you for believing in this book, even when I did not; to my soul sister, Debbie, thank you for always being a phone call away; to my teachers, Komal Minhas and Nigel Walker, thank you for guiding me to discover the strength I possessed within and providing the tools I needed to step into my truth; to Alexandra Elle, thank you for guiding me back towards my gift of writing.

A special thanks goes to my partner in life and love, Chisom, for your unwavering love and support, for your joyous spirit that you share, and for challenging me to lean into my most uncomfortable emotions to meet the parts of myself that lay buried within; and to my dear friends, Lara, Logine and Adil, for being a consistent source of joy in my life, for loving and accepting me as I am and for always rooting for me no matter what.

Thank you to countless others without whom this book would not exist; and thank you to you, the reader, for picking up this book and joining me on this part of my journey.

I appreciate you,

Samukele

Foreword

by Nigel Walker

As an avid reader and creator of poetry and inspirational writing myself, this book was a welcome exploration of the self-love journey through Sam's eyes. And yet, I felt completely seen and heard as I found myself lost in the world that her words created for me.

It's the kind of book you can read all in one sitting or flip to a random page and read just the thing you need to hear in that moment but couldn't find the words to express.

My own self-love journey started when I realized that the things about myself that I thought needed to be changed or fixed were also the things that made me unique. By sharing those parts of myself I was most afraid of, I learned to be brave with my life so other people could be brave with theirs.

And this book is such a perfect example of that.

So brew yourself a fresh pot of coffee or tea, tuck yourself in, and give yourself the gift of letting these words wash over you.

I promise you won't regret it.

- Nigel Walker

Preface

This collection of poetry and notes is a product of my growth and healing. For a long time, I felt lost and was trying so hard to find myself. I longed for someone to tell me exactly who I was and spent a lot of time talking to people, asking them for advice, and searching externally for what I should do with my life.

A dear friend took notice and said to me, "You know, no one can tell you who you are, right?" I said yes, but deep down, I don't feel I knew that at the time.

Over the following years, I entered a spiral where I got lost in defining my worth and who I was through the things that I did. I was trying so hard to prove that I was worthy because I did "stuff", but at the end of the day, all the things that I was doing weren't filling me up. They were draining me until my body said no more.

It was only when my body stepped in that I was forced to be still - to slow down and just be. How scary it was! I thought, "If I'm not doing anything, then what worth or value do I bring?"

This stillness forced me to shift my focus from the external and look deeper within myself to find what really mattered to me. I had spent a lot of time living my life the way I thought I should, doing what I thought I should be doing, saying what I thought I should be saying; while losing sight of my internal guiding voice.

The metamorphosis that accompanied the stillness was uncomfortable and unfamiliar. It felt as though everything I had known myself to be, up until that point, was false, and in order to uncover who I truly was, I had to shed all of the things and beliefs about who I thought myself to be.

As confusing as this period of my life was, over time, I found the forced stillness started to bring me peace. For the first time in a long time, I was still enough to sit with myself and just be, and, at last, that was when my internal guiding voice was able to peek through.

Now, I see that I just needed to tune into myself to get all the answers I was seeking; to meet the person I was all along.

It's been a long road of unlearning and relearning, peeling off all the masks and roles I play to reveal the real me that lives within - daily work that is painful at times but is so liberating on the best of days.

And now I know without a shadow of a doubt that all the things I spent so long looking for were already within me.

My Intention

This book was born as a result of one of the most challenging periods of my life. The pieces in this collection were created through reflections after asking myself, "What do I need to hear most right now?"

I decided to bring these writings into the world to help anyone who feels lost, like they aren't living as their true, authentic selves, or like they are afraid to share their truth and be seen - as I did.

I want you to know, I see you.

I created this collection to help you realize that you are more powerful than you know. You are a gift, and your existence helps to shape the world in a way that is so magical and can only be brought about by you alone.

All you need to do is be yourself.

Navigate this book in a way that feels right to you. That could be reading these writings in chronological order, flipping to a random page that you feel called to read, or anything in between.

No matter what you do, I know you will be guided to discover the thing you need to hear most.

May you continue to blossom.

Contents

The Egg   25

The Caterpillar   35

The Cocoon   47

The Butterfly   63

1

The Egg

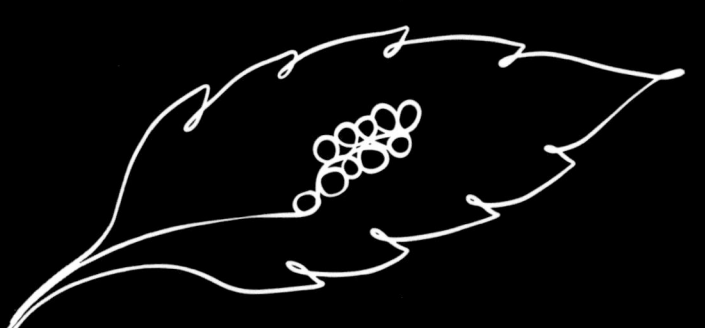

Deep breath in,

Take in the world around you.

Listen to the whispers of the Wind;
Feel her brush against your skin as she carries the
    secrets of the Universe on her breath.

Smell the air that carries notes of the river's water,
And watch the birds dart in and out of the trees,
    without a care in the world.

Get out of your head.

Life is not lived in there,
But out here.

Open your eyes to look,

And allow the beauty to surprise you.

Take off your mask.

It is okay to show people how you truly feel.

It must be exhausting to have your guard up and
....play a role all the time -
Becoming the person everyone else needs,

But yourself.

Don't lose sight of who you are.
Those who love you will stand by you no matter
....how messy, broken, or lost you may feel.

Continue to trust your inner voice, and don't let
....the world manipulate you into becoming a
....caricature of who you were born to be.

Tend to your needs first,
The world can wait.

For the stronger you are,
The brighter your light can shine.

Rest, rejuvenate and refresh,

But first,
Take off your mask.

Asking for help does not make you weak.

It shows you understand what you need in this moment to thrive.

Asking for help does not make you weak.
It allows you to share your vulnerability,
A necessary ingredient for forming the most profound connections.

Asking for help does not make you weak.
It is your oxygen mask when you are drowning, creating space for you to breathe.

Asking for help does not make you weak.

It makes you human.

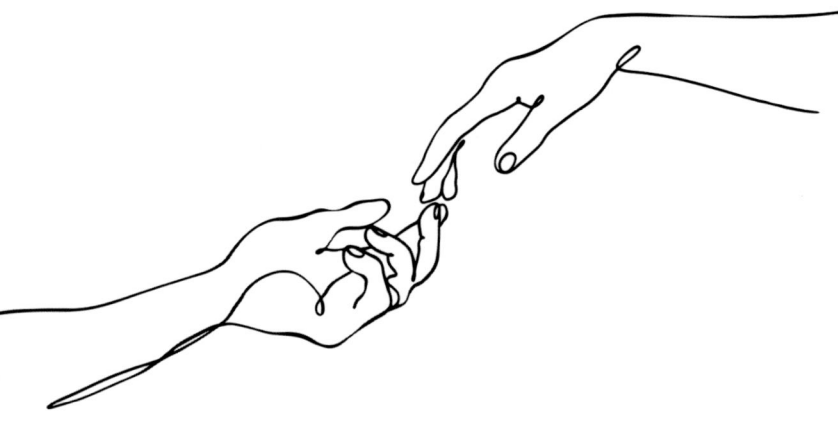

You are capable of creating your wildest dreams.

Don't fall victim to the limitations that Society has
 put on you.
You have the power to rise above the voice in your
 head that whispers doubts and insecurities into
 your ears.

Remember, you are whole.
You were made complete, and you are perfect as
 you are.

Your work doesn't define your worth.
It is only a reflection of what you believe you are
 capable of.
Dominate that voice until it also believes the truth -
That you are worthy,

Simply because you are.

To truly love others,

You must first love yourself.
Have a complete acceptance
Of everything that makes you,
You.

Honour yourself,
Yes, even the parts that you deny;
The ones you have cast away to the shadows -
They are you.

Yet, they make you no lesser a person,
And make you no less loveable -
They are you.

By denying parts of yourself,
You deny yourself love;
And to truly love others,

You must first love yourself.

The land of Should

Is where joy goes to die.

A graveyard overflowing with tombstones
Suppressing the muffled screams of dreams

Unrealized.

The duality of life is

Light cannot exist without darkness -
And the darker it is,
The brighter the light can shine.

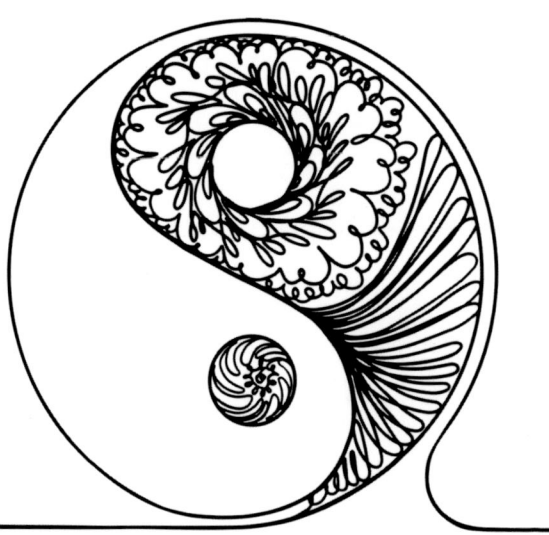

Why are you always seeking to be doing something?

Don't you know your worth far exceeds that which
 you accomplish with your hands?
Or your mind or your mouth?

You are worth more than the diamonds, emeralds,
 and pearls of the earth
Combined.

Do you know why?
Because you are.

All you need to do?
Just be.

Everything in the world

Is always in motion.
When you wish for things to remain the same,
It goes against the natural order of things
And so begins the suffering.

2
The Caterpillar

Perfection

Is just an illusion that tells you you are less than
 who you are.
When you give your all to everything you do,
Know that it is enough.

Perfection is cunning,
Tirelessly working to deceive you from realizing
 She is a destination that never arrives.

You will never return to yesterday,
Or arrive at tomorrow;

You only ever have right now to do your best -

So take action fearlessly,
And know that it is enough.

Have you ever had the feeling that something was so blatantly obvious,

But no one else could see it?
Where you start to question your own sanity,
But don't dare to point it out?
That thing, which only you can see, and everyone
    else seems to be oblivious to,
Is your perspective.

It is the gift that only you can bring into the world.

Your ability to open people's eyes to what appears
    to be invisible to them, and is blatant to you,
Is the light you shine on the Universe.

Don't let the sea of blind men stifle your flame -
You were born to shine!
Brilliantly, vividly and unapologetically.

You were meant to be here at this moment in time.
Your light pierces the veil of darkness that has
    shrouded the eyes of the world, and in so doing,
Allows others to rediscover their light.

Nothing in this world is a coincidence,
And your existence is the ripple that triggers the
    waves of change.

The wandering cloud knows its course.

Continuously growing and shrinking along her
    voyage across the sky,
But never losing course.

She may merge with other clouds;
Enjoying their company for a while,
But she never loses sight of her vision.

For coordinates of her destiny are divinely
    programmed in her atoms.

Joy is always around the corner,

Just waiting to be found.

The garden of your mind

Deserves the utmost care.

Water it with compassion,
And fertilize the soil with words of affirmation.

Be fierce in weeding out thoughts of self-loathing,
And lovingly prune away ideas that bring doubt.

This will cultivate the knowing of who you truly are
To grow in its place;
Letting love

Bloom.

Every new second

Provides a fresh start.
It's never too late
To start again.

An ocean of dandelions,

Some have just begun life, sprouting freshly from the ground,

Others are fully-grown and proudly bare their yellow petals for all to see.

Still, others have matured into fragile white clouds
Which could blow away into the sky without a moment's notice,

To start their lives anew as little seeds
In lands afar.

Do what you can,

When you can.

Consistency means coming back, even when you fall off.

You are not a robot,

You are Human.

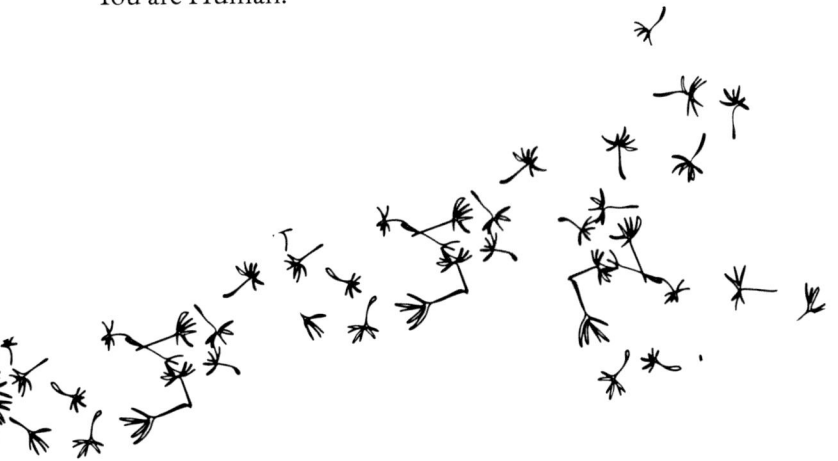

Joy is found in the little things.

It's in the Sun's warming touch as She kisses your skin at sunset;

It's in the intricacy of the clouds on overcast days;

It's in the melodies of the birds as they exchange sweet symphonies across the trees;

It's in the way the river laps at the rocks ashore;

It's in the gentle tapping of the raindrops as they massage your skin.

And just as quickly as the rain comes, she goes,
Making way for the Sun to shine through her droplets,

Breathing life into a magnificent rainbow.

It is a choice that is made in every moment;
And it is knowing there are better days ahead,

For joy is not a destination.

Sift through the mess

To find the beauty.

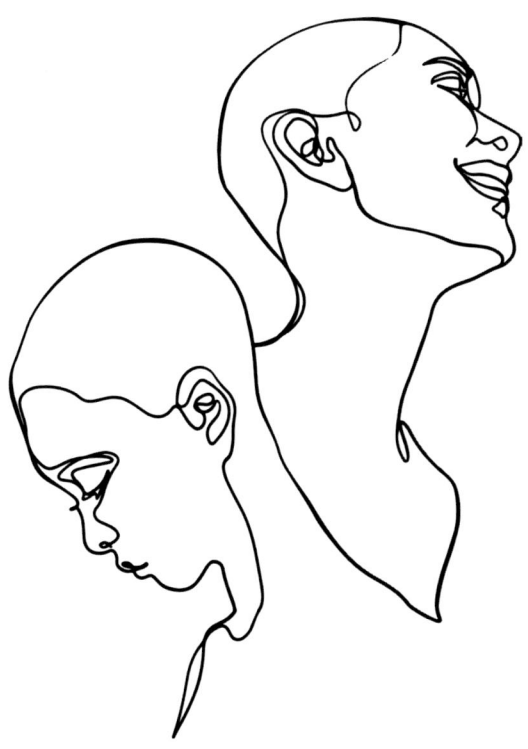

3

The Cocoon

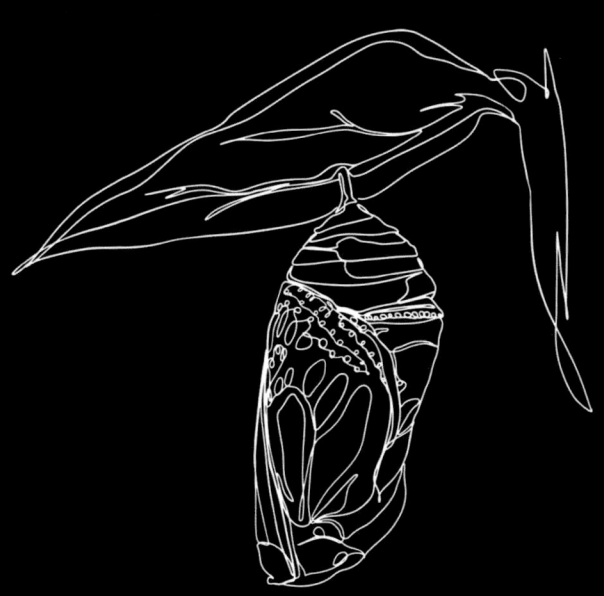

The Sun is always shining.

Even when Her rays are obscured,
Her beauty permeates through the blanket of
 clouds that attempts to smother Her glory.
Look how the trees still grow in Her absence.
They rest in the peace of knowing that Her rays
 will radiate on them once more.

The Sun is always shining,
Even as She sets over the horizon.
Although Her dazzling orb is beyond view behind
 the mountains,
She leaves behind evidence of Her presence
 through the bright orange, pink and purple
 hues She paints across the sky.

She is always shining,
Even when the Moon provides relief from Her
 daily duty,
Taking His place as the eye in the sky over the
 night shift.
Look at the stars! How they reflect Her brilliance.

And when the night meets its end,
The stars will fade away -
One by one, until they are no more.
Because they know they could never match Her.

And just as the trees, the flowers, and the grass trust
    the Sun will always shine down on them,
So too should you, friend.
Know that this, too, shall pass.
And the Sun will shine on you once more.

It is those

That have intimately known deep despair,
Who possess the gift of bringing forth the light.

It is in the hidden crevices of the darkness
That a profound understanding of the power of
   light is forged.

Those who walk this path are entrusted with
   bringing the light into the world,

For only they know
What lies beyond the veil of luminescence.

The secret to finding yourself

Lies in the complete and unconditional acceptance
 of everything you are.

Yet, you manipulate and strain your being through
 a sieve
Whose intricately-woven mesh is made up of all
 the ideas of who you think you should be.

You are so much more than the diluted product
 that sifts through to the other side.

If only you could see the light you possessed -
You would never let any part of your beautiful
 being pass through a filter

Before it entered into the world.

Show up,

Even with the fear,
And trust that the Universe
Will take care of the rest.

You have the complete blueprint for your life.

Only you know what will make you happy
But to live and experience the joy of doing what
    you love,
You need courage.
The courage to walk away from what Society told
    you you wanted,
And the audacity to own your path.

You already have the answers you seek -
They may be hidden in your childhood dreams
    and aspirations,
Or the hobbies you let go of at the price of
    becoming an "adult."
Or even the things you admire most in others;
It is all within you.

And only you have the power to unearth the gift
    buried so deep within.

Remember this:
You are the only expert on your life.
Everything you feel, think, and experience is valid;
And no one can tell you otherwise.

Let that knowledge give you the courage to walk
    into the life you were meant to lead -
One that brings you continuous peace
And never-ending joy.

Growth is not linear.

Like the river's flow,
It meanders.
Waxing and waning,
Racing and slowing.

Yet it is always moving.

Even when it appears still on the surface,
There is a world of activity bubbling below,
Just waiting to burst forth -
Given the right conditions.

All that it takes is patience.

Sometimes

The discomfort of remaining as we were is so great
It forces us to grow;

As the caterpillar must shed the skin that once
 housed its identity.

It is in the quiescent chrysalis -
The caterpillar's protective vessel of unseen growth,
 pain, and healing,

That metamorphosis occurs;

To transform the humble caterpillar into the
 majestic butterfly

It was made to be.

The healing journey

Oscillates between moments of pure knowing that liberate you,
And moments of self-doubt that are crippling.

No matter what,
Stay the course!

Over time, those moments of knowing will grow longer and longer,

Until that is all you experience.

The rain isn't always as scary as it seems.

Let it fall on your face without resistance,

Washing away your fears and troubles on its
 journey to meet the Earth.

It is a friend,
Here to remind you of the power of surrender.

When it begins to fall harder,
Dance without a care in the world!

For heaven weeps
When you take yourself too seriously.

The gifts of time and perspective

Will illuminate your path
And give meaning to your journey.

You don't have to understand now,
Just trust that there is a reason for what you are
 going through.

One day it will all make sense
And you'll look back at the difficult times,
Grateful for all of the twists and turns that

Shaped you into who you became.

Change.

A crucial part of any evolution.

For that which stays the same will inevitably erode.
Just as the green summer leaves turn orange and
 shed before the winter
To make way for fresh life in the spring,

And begin the cycle anew.

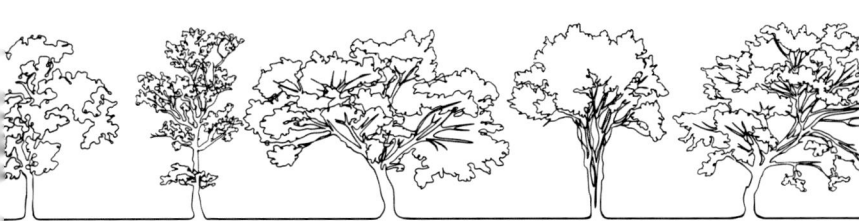

The seemingly disconnected parts of your life,

Make up the important plots in your story

So move when you feel compelled to move
In the direction that you are drawn to

Your job is just to take action
And not to worry about the rest.

Like the rain,

Emotions come and go.
Sometimes the storm is relentless,
Pouring down and lasting for weeks,
Other times it is a drizzle,
Producing light showers that dissipate quickly in
    the wind.
Through it all,
The sun remains constant,
Always shining no matter what
Looking for opportunities to pierce through
    the clouds,
Even just for a moment,
To remind you she is always there.

Not everyday will go as planned.

Try again tomorrow.

4

The Butterfly

Metamorphosis.

The shedding of the old to create space for the new;
The bending, breaking, and burning
To recreate life that is stronger
And can only be forged through destruction.

You are the Universe,

The water that flows gently through streams,
And rages across rapids;
The wind that whispers in the valleys,
And roars atop the mountains;
The flame that glows in the dying embers,
And ravages forests;
The fine sand on the beach,
And the gravity-defying boulders on the
    water's edge.
The Sun that burns fiercely at noon,
And the stars that twinkle at midnight.

You are the Universe,
And the Universe is you.

Don't deny your gifts -

They are the key
To unlocking the life of your dreams.

Celebrate yourself.

You've grown so much,
Look around; it is evident in the smallest things -

When you make breakfast a priority,
When you drink that extra glass of water before
    bed at night,
When you bathe and cleanse your body,
When you take time to be still,
When you say no when you mean no,
When you allow yourself to laugh and be joyful in
    each passing moment.

All these little decisions that you have been making
    consistently have created a monumental shift.
Look up and see how all these minute steps have
    carried you further than you imagined.

Keep going; I see your progress.
Keep choosing joy,
Keep choosing yourself,

And watch how you blossom.

Peace is

Watching the cotton-shaped clouds travel across the blue sky.

The setting Sun piercing through the dark clouds' veil to bathe the earth in her light.

The clouds breaking into various forms as they complete their journey to God-Knows-Where.

A woman dancing with her child; a bunny jumping over a fence; a mouse watching it all unfold.

And just when the clouds seem to have taken their final shape, they transform, yet again.

The clouds' journey, like life — with no beginning, a perpetual middle and unspecified end —

Shapes, shifts, and continuously evolves to serve a higher purpose,

Known only to the clouds.

Nothing compares to the joy

Of becoming
More yourself

The Universe makes no mistakes.

You were chosen
As the vessel to bring forth creations
Planted in the fertile soil of your mind.

Your Truth

Is your shield and sword,
Protecting you from the spaces that are not meant
　　for you,
And drawing you closer to the people that make
　　your soul sing.

It is the compass,
Navigating you towards your destiny,
And the path that holds
Your purpose.

Share it without fear,
Without shame,
And without doubt.

You were not made for every place and every one,
So let your truth guide you towards
Unconditional love, acceptance and understanding.

You are love;

Pure, beautiful, and perfect.
If you ever believe otherwise,
You have forgotten who you are.

You are love;
Pure, beautiful, and perfect.
And just as the migrating birds have a
    predetermined path,
Etched into the strands of your DNA is your
    journey.

You are love;
Pure, beautiful, and perfect.
Let your light shine and strip away the darkness
To illuminate the lives of others who have
    forgotten this truth.

To know peace

Is to know yourself,
And to be still,
Is to return home.

Self-care is self-love.

Taking care of your mind, body, and spirit
Signals to yourself that you are worthy,

You matter,

And you are loved -

Always.

You have infinite power,

If only you knew the well of strength you possess,
You'd never second guess yourself again.
Keep going.
Trust.

You can always find home

Within yourself.

Thank you, friend, for choosing to experience this book. I created it as part of my healing journey and decided to share it because I realized that these words could be the medicine that someone else may need.

It has been the most challenging and joyous road for me to bring this book to you and I am so grateful that it found you.

I hope this book touched and offered some tenderness to the parts of your soul that needed it, and I trust you were able to find the thing you needed to hear most.

May this book always find you in your times of need.

We are all butterflies, at some point on our journey toward self-actualization, and I hope that you can find the courage to trust in the gentle call of your inner guiding voice.

About the Author

Samukele Ncube is a Creator whose gift lies in writing. As a recovering perfectionist and overachiever, writing has been the cornerstone of her journey towards healing and in learning self-love.

In a world that constantly tells us who we should be, she is a strong believer that we all have the answers that we seek to live out our life's purpose and strives to help others rediscover their internal guiding voice through her work.

Things You Need to Hear Most is her debut collection of poetry and notes, rooted in self-love, and has allowed to her to embrace her gift of writing for the first time, while also offering others healing through words that she needed on her darkest days.

Through her work, Samukele strives to give her readers reassurance that they matter and they have something important to bring into the world. She aims to give them the courage to follow their own unique paths by listening to the gentle guidance of their inner guiding voices, and tune out the noise of worldly expectations.

Connect with Samukele through her website, www.samukelencube.com, or by scanning the QR code below using your phone camera.

Connect with Samukele

 www.samukelencube.com

 sam@samukelencube.com

 @thesamncube

 @thesamncube

 @thesamncube

 @thesamukelencube

 Samukele Ncube

In Your Own Words

Things You Need to Hear Most

Today I Need to Hear:

Today I Need to Hear:

Things You Need to Hear Most

Today I Need to Hear:

Today I Need to Hear:

Things You Need to Hear Most

Today I Need to Hear:

Today I Need to Hear:

www.ingramcontent.com/pod-product-compliance
Lightning Source LLC
Chambersburg PA
CBRC090905080526
44589CB00009B/82